TO KEEP FROM UNDRESSING

AISHA SHARIF

Cover design by Liz Kay

Book design by Liz Kay

ISBN: 978-0-9897837-6-7

Published by Spark Wheel Press

TO KEEP FROM UNDRESSING

AISHA SHARIF

SPARK WHEEL PRESS
OMAHA, NE

TABLE OF CONTENTS

SECTION 3

SECTION 4

SECTION 5

SECTION 1

Why I Can Dance Down a Soul-Train Line in Public and Still Be Muslim

My Islam be black.
Not that "Don't-like-white-folks"
kind of black. I mean my Islam be
who I am—black, born and raised
Muslim in Memphis, Tennessee
by parents who converted
black. It be my 2 brothers
and 2 sisters Muslim too
black, praying at Masjid Al-Muminun,
formally Temple #55,
located at 4412 South Third Street
in between the Strip Club
and the Save-A-Lot black.
My Islam be bean pie black,
sisters cooking fish dinners
after Friday prayer black,
brothers selling them newspapers
on the front steps black, everybody
struggling to pay the mortgage back
black.

My Islam be Sister Clara Muhammad School
black, starting each day
with the pledge of allegiance
then prayer & black history
black. It be blue jumpers
over blue pants, girls pulling bangs out
of their hijabs to look cute
black. My Islam be black & Somali
boys and girls, grades 2 through 8,
learning Arabic in the same classroom
cuz we only had one classroom
black. It be everybody wearing a coat inside
cuz the building ain't got no heat
black.

My Islam be the only Muslim girl
at a public high school
where everybody COGIC asking sidewise,
What church you go to?
black. It be me trying to explain hijab
black, *No, I don't have cancer. No,*
I'm not a nun. No, I don't take showers
with my scarf on. No, I'm not
going to hell cuz I haven't accepted
Jesus Christ as my Lord and Savior
black. My Islam be riding on the city bus
next to crackheads and dope boys
black, be them whispering black,
be me praying they don't follow me home
black.

My Islam don't hate Christians
cuz all my aunts, cousins,
and grandparents be Christian
black. It be joining them for Easter
brunch cuz family still family
black. My Islam be Mus-Diva
black, head wrapped up,
feathered and jeweled black. It be me
two-stepping in hijab and four-inch heels
cuz dancing be in my bones
black.

My Islam be just as good as any Arab's.
It be me saying, *No, I ain't gonna pray*
in a separate room cuz I'm a woman
black. And, *Don't think I can't recite Quran too.*
Now pray on that black!

My Islam be universal
cuz black be universal.
It be Morocco and Senegal,
India and Egypt. My Islam
don't need to be Salafi
or Sufi. It don't have to be
blacker than yours black.
My Islam just has to be.

I.

He was a light-skinned woman's son.
An only child. Raised in Jack & Jill,
photo ops for the NAACP.
Boarding schooled at Wooster.
Escorted southern belles
to cotillions. A doctor's son—first black
ear, nose, and throat doctor
in Memphis. A doctor's grandson too—
one of a few black OBGYNs in the city
at the turn of the century.
Scored perfectly on his SAT
then glided right into Yale
at 16. His name was William Oscar Speight III.
Billy for short.

II.

She was the daughter of an electrician
and a light-skinned homemaker.
Catholic schooled in the suburbs of St. Louis,
working to be a nutritionist, a Mrs., a mother.
Met Billy and got champagned—
dinner jackets and quartets on his parent's patio,
a full wedding mass at St. Mary Magdalen,
wedding pictures in *Jet*,
Don Cornelius at the reception, the envy
of all of her friends. Got a husband she loved
no matter the money, an MBA man
accounting at W. R. Grace & Co.,
gin and rings, roses and cocktails,
Christmas at the Peabody Club.
Help every week.
Her name was Brenda Witt, then
Brenda Speight, happily.

III.

Then came his father's sudden death
and the pressure of legacy.
Billy had one kid then another
then questions like, **What's it worth anyways?**
He visited a mosque, got freedom
from routines and make-believe.
Then was laid-off and felt the struggle
and thrill of making it
for the first time—ever. He studied Qur'an,
started eating rice and lamb
on the kitchen floor, selling incense and oils,
substitute teaching. Walked out of his circle
of friends, those men at the bar
smoking Montecristo cigars
like his father and changed his name
to Rashad, Rashad Sharif, proudly.

IV.

And she, out of awe and love of family,
took on overtime and worry,
a hijab and Arabic classes, bills
and broke-down station wagons,
her parents' questions. Fashioned a home
with Arabic calligraphy but no pictures.
Learned to fast during Ramadan, sunup
to sunset, settled on sending their kids
to the Islamic School, still remembering
the parties, the clubs, and the recognition
of it all—how easily they could have kept it up.
Changed her last name—again—
from Speight to Sharif—
but kept Brenda for herself.

The Learner's Objective: To Simplify Faith

Step 1. Weigh pros and cons

old ways : new ways
old ways = club + pork + alcohol + foreplay
new ways = 5 prayers + Ramadan + Eid + charity

$$\frac{\text{Christianity} - \text{ianity}}{\text{old ways}} = \text{Islam}$$

Step 2. Shift between beliefs

$$\frac{\text{Christianity} - \text{ianity}}{\text{old ways}} \text{ +/- you} = \text{Islam +/- you}$$

Step 3. Substitute for variable

ianity = the trinity + Christmas + Easter + cross

$$\frac{\text{Christianity} - \text{(the trinity + Christmas + Easter + cross)}}{\text{old ways}} \text{ +/- you} = \text{Islam +/- you}$$

Step 4. Simplify

$$\frac{\text{Christ}}{\text{old ways}} \text{ +/- you} = \text{Islam +/- you}$$

Step 5. Multiply both sides by new ways

$$(\text{new ways}) (\frac{\text{Christ}}{\text{old ways}} \text{ +/- you}) = (\text{Islam +/- you}) (\text{new ways})$$

Step 6. Substitute for variable

old ways = club + pork + alcohol + foreplay
new ways= 5 prayers + Ramadan + Eid + charity

(5 prayers + Ramadan + Eid + charity) (<u>Christ</u> +/- you)
$$\frac{}{\text{the club} + \text{pork} + \text{alcohol} + \text{foreplay}}$$
= (Islam +/- you) (5 prayers + Ramadan + Eid + charity)

Step 7. Distribute new ways

(new ways)(<u>Christ</u>) +/- (new) you) = (Islam)(new) +/- (you)(new ways)
$$\frac{}{\text{old ways}}$$

Step 8. Cancel the fraction

(new ways)(Christ) +/- (new) you) = (Islam)(new) +/- (you)(new ways)

Step 9. Review your product

Christ +/- new you = Islam2 +/- new you

Step 10. Substitute you

      a.   Christ +/- Mark = Islam^2 +/- Malik
      b.   Christ +/- Keisha = Islam^2 +/- Khadijah

Note: A fundamental theorem of Islam is Christ + his teachings = Islam

Challenge Step: Graph your figure

a full beard	a draped scarf
polish-free nails	covered legs

Conversion Residuals

You are the two daughters born
before your father's conversion,
who were pictured standing in front
of a Christmas tree playing Santa
before you knew you could no longer believe
in that kind of faith. You are the elder daughters
who retain your father's birth name,
Speight, remnants of a halted line,
the only two bridges to memory—
to your father's prep school,
his mother's opera gloves,
his father's practice,
to Black society.

You think of your father's trips to the mosque,
the Arabic of his new last name, Sharif,
and breathe knowing that yours has kept you
in sororities, Southern Black colleges,
everyone's recollection.
If it weren't for your name,
old folks would never remember,
You're Billy's kids.

You think, if a man comes along
you'll hyphenate your name
or simply won't change it.
That won't do.
You are women.
You cannot carry names forever.
With each child, you'll deflect,
defer to your husband.
You are women.
Men's names take precedent
in any faith.
So, you stay single,
stone pillars of history.

IF MY PARENTS HADN'T CONVERTED: QUESTIONS & ANSWERS PT. I

1.   What would my name be?

        Marian Elizabeth Speight

2.   Who would have held me during my baptism?

        My father,
        standing by the fountain
        of holy water
        in the foyer of the
        Immaculate Conception,
        would have cradled me
        in folds of his left arm,
        his right hand resting
        gently over my heart.

3.   Cheerleader or gymnast?

        A gymnast — what freedom
        to run and flip
        to twist myself
        out of questions
        then dance
        with a smile
        head tilted back
        across an open floor.

4.   Who would have taken me to my cotillion?

        A thin, light-skinned boy
        named Harold or Samuel
        who lives on South Parkway East,

whose grandparents
knew my grandparents
years ago at LeMoyne Owen College
or maybe who marched with Dr. King
during his last visits to Memphis.

5.   How short would my prom dress have been?

Just short enough
to reveal
my knees.
A lady
is still a lady.

6.   How many boyfriends would I have had?

3
or 4.
Harold
or Samuel.
John, the summer fling
from the Racquet Club,
& Joey, the pre-med
from IU.

To My Muslim Father

If I was seven, I could dance for you,
parade and spin my pink parasol.
You would laugh, call me, *Beautiful girl*.
Back then, I strutted on tables
when teachers weren't looking,
wore shorts and parted my hair.
I was a junior majorette. I batted my eyes
and twirled an oversized baton.
I had lots of boyfriends.

To my dismay, I grew to be a woman.
You said it was time I hide the girl
underneath long sleeves and silk scarves.
You sent me to the Muslim school
where girls wore white leggings
under ankle-length blue jumpers.
I wrapped a scarf over my hair.
You said it sat like a crown,
but it gripped my head,
left red bumps around the edges.
I would twirl my finger around loose strands,
tap my feet to old dance routines.

You ignored me for a week
the time I drew a heart on my ankle while
your sons did everything under your eye.
I dreamed about getting you back,
wearing fishnets, smoking cigarettes,
trading my scarf for a scarlet beret.

But I studied your face and saw myself.
I knew you were making a model of me.
I added in rhythms of Arabic prayers,
introduced myself as your daughter.
Faith had become my ticket to you,

to that beautiful girl still dancing in my sleeves.
I began to love you unconsciously. Yes,
father, you made a Muslim out of me.

LAYL-TUL-QADR (THE NIGHT OF POWER)

Women enter through the back of the mosque,
cut off from men by thin, white-laced curtains.
They rest their backs and hips,
sore from standing in hot kitchens
over pots of lamb stew.
My mother is somewhere among them.

Tonight is Layl-tul-Qadr,
the night better than a thousand months.
The adults will spend the night
praying until dawn appears.
I will doodle, stroll the halls, and watch them—
hungry, thirsty, ready to eat up blessings.

The women sit on red rugs in the musalla
whispering in black hijabs.
I walk, bite my lip, and guess
which woman is the one I see uncovered
at home, the woman who laughs
when I touch the mole on her collar bone.
I can feel the women inspect me with their eyes.
My mother calls with a finger. I run to her side.
The thikr is starting soon, she says.

When I was five, I stared at silhouettes
of men in front, bending in prayer.
I could run and sit on my father's lap.
He smiled when I pointed at men
with salt and pepper beards.
Now, the women must do.
For my birthday last month,
my mother gave me a training bra
and a white hijab.

The women sit in a circle.
My mother pulls me in.

You need this, she says.
Twenty black women, mirrors of myself.
They finger beads, some strung with red thread,
others with green.
A woman begins,
Ya Allah.
The others join.
Ya Allah.
I bite my nails. The volume rises.
Ya Allah.
My mother nudges my leg. I call up,
Ya Allah.

The women's bodies move
side to side, forward and back as if
rocking a child to sleep. I begin to sway.
My mother's thumb rubs my palm.
Her skin is soft.
Ya Allah.

We chant one thousand times
and fill the air with prayer.
Ya Allah. Words push against walls,
seep through the white curtain
and into the men's section.
My throat is dry, eyes half open.
My voice sounds an echo of itself,
as if it has been swallowed
by the others.

And then a woman claps her hands.
The swaying ends; the volume sinks.
My mother hugs and kisses me,
and I hear my voice,
Ya Allah, strangely full.

H*IJAB*

~*after A. Van Jordan*

Hijab (hi jeb) (n.) 1. A screen or curtain that separates a space or establishes a threshold: As in, Mary pulled the *hijab* across the room and cut off her husband. Why shouldn't she have a space of her own? 2. A covering or hiding of the truth: Joseph saw straight through his wife's *hijab*; despite her distance, her constant cold shoulder, she loved him. How could she pretend she wasn't combing him through her head? 3. A metaphoric partition separating the sacred and the profane: Every Sunday morning, Mary crawled from under Joseph, showered, dressed, grabbed her book, and left for worship. No matter his sweet whispers, Mary kept up her *hijab*. It tore Joseph to pieces, her devotion to a man more complex than he. 4. A system of behavior, modesty or respect: Each morning Joseph stood in the mirror, inspecting his *hijab*—bloodshot eyes, purple-brown lips, smoked of color. What kind of man was he? Eclipsed by his wife's *hijab*, Joseph could never fashion one bright enough to display. 5. A way of covering the body, especially the hair, out of modesty: Mary looked through old wedding pictures—the veil, the satin gloves, her train sweeping the floor—the *hijab* of it all. Marriage was formality, a way to silence gossip. Joseph could never complete her. But she did it because she loved God. She loved Him more than any man could.

Under Veils

At 17, Sister Agnes left her lover for the veil.
His touch still lingers. Her habit is of no avail.

Please, no more of your poems. My love—
a shadow, autumn's red veiling.

Men dream of hijabis. Hair pours
rum into their hands, drunkenness unveiled.

A man's touch is smoothly twisted—hair
around a finger. When hijabis love, they love in veils.

Kiss the dip of my collarbone. My father
will not see. It is night beneath this veil.

God, place your hands above my eyes. Lower
my gaze. Don't let me see through your veil.

A'ishah tasted Qur'an on the Prophet's breath.
When she exhaled, Arabic crawled across her veil.

ALTAR

The sisters at Mt. St. Scholastica have offed
their habits. They cut their hair and dress
in pants, line their halls with women
who have stepped out of this world
of men. Oh, to be so bold
to create your own holy space,
never batting an eye or falling
off of a cliff.

After Brother Mustafa drilled our daily calisthenics,
we were free to play, to forget
the morning's word problem and black history lesson.
All of us, grades 3 through 8,
huddled outside that large brick building,
once home to the KKK, and picked teams
for a game that didn't discriminate. We took turns
being captains. Wali, the eldest boy in school,
could make the ball glide across gravel
and then fly up and linger for a second.
He knew placement, how to aim
in between defenders, give full nelsons to his brother,
then turn around and lead zhur prayer.
Mansoor and Yusuf, stocky boys, couldn't read
Arabic and didn't care. They knew how to throw hard
to 1st base, laughing as the ball bounced off our heads.
Then there was Willie, a tall boy who could leap straight,
snatch your ball before you could reach home,
the boy Sister Rosie called on to grab a broom
to swat this week's pigeons that squeezed
through the holes in the roof.

And there were girls like Khadijah
who could deceive you with her small frame and outrun
Sabir and Steven, a girl who never let herself believe
she couldn't lead her own team.
And then there was Zola, whose momma was Ajanaku
and didn't trust those white people and their schools—
Zola, the girl who would stop by a defender,
catch her breath and call out their momma,
then say **Allahuakbar, losers!** as she g-walked home.
No one could tell her she wasn't Muslim.
To play kickball, we had to judge
when to stay on base and when to steal home
like Rashad who snuck out of school one afternoon

to buy hot chips at the neighborhood Save-A-Lot.
He could fake so well you'd actually believe
he knew that surah he was mouthing during Islamic Studies.
But it was Ayoob who really memorized the 99 names of Allah,
only to forget the last 87 after going to public school
and making friends with boys who had beepers.

At our school, black skin glistened from sun.
We thought nothing of returning inside
to hot rooms, extension cords, and floor fans
set to HIGH. We'd wipe off kickball sweat
and try to answer Brother Mustafa's question,
Why is water wet? never knowing
he never wanted an answer, just our engagement
with something deeper than ourselves.
We'd stopped playing the dozens in bathroom mirrors
when the adhan was called, rush to stand toe to toe
in a prayer line ignoring tattered carpets, holes in socks,
and torn pockets in jumpers. We were black kids
who prayed in Arabic and learned that our inheritance
was never gold domes and minarets,
but a muddied black and white ball rolled right at us,
free to float into air, ready to turn and twist
into something that could be caught by willing arms.

SECTION 2

AFTER SCHOOL ON THE CITY BUS, MEMPHIS, TN

I. What The Boy Said To Me:

you ain't saved if you
don't know jezuz, you god-damned
mutha fuckin muzlum

II. What I Heard The Boy Say To Me:

you ain't saved
you ain't saved
you ain't saved
you muzlum
you don't know
you don't know
you don't know
jezuz
you god-damned
you god-damned
you god-damned
you muzlum
jezuz
jezuz
jezuz
you muzlum
muzlum
muzlum
a mutha fuckin muzlum
you ain't saved
you don't know
you god-damned
jezuz
muzlum
jezuz
muzlum

muzlum
a mutha fuckin muzlum
you don't know
you ain't saved
god-damned you
jezuz
ain't saved you
don't you know
god damned you
don't you know
god ain't you

III. What I Wanted to Say To The Boy:

muslims know god
muslims know god
muslims know god
ain't damned us
god
jesus
muslims
god don't know
god don't know
god don't know
saved
mutha fuckin saved
god know
muslims
god know
jesus
jesus know
god
jesus know
muslims

muslims know
jesus
muslims know
god
jesus
muslims
jesus
god
don't you know
jesus ain't god
jesus ain't god
jesus ain't god
muslims
god
jesus
don't you know
god-damn it
jesus a muslim
jesus a muslim
jesus a muslim
a mutha fuckin muslim

IV. What I Actually Said To The Boy:

Nothing.

7.   Would I pray the rosary slow or fast?

>   Slow—with a breath taken
>   after each bead
>   long enough to reflect
>   on each mystery.

8.   Would I sing in the choir?

>   Only if
>   my sisters sang
>   with me.

9.   Our Christmas tree—pine or synthetic?

>   Pine. Only the real thing
>   for my mother
>   who would ornament it
>   with champagne-hued
>   glass globes,
>   thread ribbons
>   between each bough
>   and ask my father
>   to top it
>   with a silent-night
>   gold angel
>   passed down
>   from her grandmother.

10.   What would sausage & ham taste like?

              Nothing
              out of the ordinary.

11.   How many Muslims would I actually befriend?

TO THE WHITE BOY WHO PULLED OFF MY HIJAB IN 7TH GRADE GYM

Every morning you sat on those bleachers,
dirty brown hair, Green Day t-shirt,
ripped jeans, so desperate to screw
your parents' money away. Poor thing.
You couldn't accept Coach Bell yelling at you—
change into gym shorts, bare your pretty pale legs,
get in line, run faster, shoot straighter
stop being a wimp—while I got to run
in long sleeves, jump hurdles
in sweat pants, sit out of flag football
the whole month of Ramadan,
got to pray in the principal's office,
read my Qur'an during study hall.
I defied rules in plain sight. In Latin class,
I emerged as Artemis, virgin goddess
of the hunt, sacred guard of chastity,
bow and arrow in hand.
I couldn't be grasped. Sometimes,
I'd catch you leaning on the goal post,
arms folded, staring green-eyed right at me.

That Thursday, you decided to figure me out.
Strolled pass me and my girlfriends on the mats
and smiled. You had a chipped tooth.
I smiled back. A white boy. Never knew
a white boy. At the Islamic School, boys were black.
They prayed in front, never talked to girls
unless they were their sisters, and became men
we'd grow to marry. But not you—
so MTV. I laid my weapons down.
You walked behind me, kneeled,
and set your trap. Pretended to tie your shoe,
rose, then grabbed my shoulder. I was caught.
Placed your other hand on my head,
snatched my hijab and ran. I screamed

as if someone had cut me,
placed my hands on my head
to stop the bleeding.
Turned to find you standing stiff,
grin slowly leaving your face: my hair,
pulled into a simple ponytail, bare
to all—black boys, white boys. They were pointing,
ooo-ing at what you revealed. Me.
Naked. I couldn't breathe.

I ran for the locker room, ashamed,
collapsed on the shower floor, crying.
How could I leave
when everyone had just seen me?
The Qur'an says, **Believers should lower their gaze.**
They should turn from the desire to see
what shouldn't be seen.
I had wanted to see myself
that entire year, turned away imaginings
of my hair in your hand, skin
a shade lighter than my own—
a white boy, never knew a white boy.
I tried to keep it under wraps.
You couldn't let me, could you?

I wanted revenge like in the Prophet's day:
chase you down, grab you
from behind, tear out your tongue,
cut off your hands, blind your fucking eyes.
But what would my father say?
Away on pilgrimage, he was begging
forgiveness for what he had seen, pleading God
forgive those men who, months before,
let their rage blow up a tower in Manhattan.
How could I be a believer

and wish to see that kind of rage?
I had to forgive you.

After class, I walked out of the locker room
arms over my head, make-shift scarf.
Coach Bell handed me my hijab
and sent us to the Vice Principal's office
where you confessed, said you didn't know
it was such a big deal. You were suspended
then paddled—repeatedly. I didn't stay to watch
but heard you scream through the door,
grasping hard your punishment.
I wanted to turn and scream back,
Stop! He didn't know what he was doing.
But the door's hard lines reminded me
this was out of my control. I couldn't keep you
from justice.

A HIJAB OF MY OWN

Every Friday, I wrestle with it—
my kinky hair,
the need to make it slick like Arab girls'.
Hijab never glides over puffs and twists.
To enter their mosque, I must pin the ends
below my chin, pretend
the silk doesn't snag, and my ears don't burn,
skin rubbed red. In their mosque,
women sit behind a lace curtain,
drape hijab over their heads and chests.
These women are from everywhere except here.
An Arab asks where my parents were born.
I must be from somewhere too. Maybe Somalia.
No, America, I reply.
She can't understand. She asks my name.
I say *I-sha*, never *I-e-sha*.
I am what is easy for them.
I-sha....the Prophet's wife...
Masha'allah I-sha.
They bless my name, kiss me
on each cheek, offer *Salaams*. I itch
to push back the fabric, wrap it like Badu,
cloth spiraled around black hair
spreading up and out—
my hijab's natural cushion.

ACCENT

You think while drinking Arabic coffee,
at the house of your Saudi friends,
that you have been embraced,
that they don't see your black skin.

You think of how you've helped them
revise their essays for their business classes
at IU, how you've taught them
what a Hoosier is and how to pronounce
the word cousin with an s, not a z
like you say with your family in Memphis.

You think of how you spoke up for them
after 9/11. So, you're confused when they snicker
after you ask, **What time is prayer at the masjid?**
They remind you it's **mahs-jid**, not **maas-jid**.
You thank them for their lesson
and think of how everyone back home
spoke like you spoke.

You wonder what other Arabic words
you speak come out black,
how your **As-Salaam Alaikum**
sounds more like **Slam-lakum**,
how you pronounce the Arabic letter **ain**
like ain't, as in **There ain't nothing
I can't do as good as you.**

You always held your breath
when your 11th grade English teacher,
Mrs. Mulherin, called students to read
out loud. Each time she made you stand
and face the class when you said **aks**
rather than **ask**. You learned
to switch tongues

around your cousins,
that it was ok to say, *I ain't tell nobody.*
But you'd always say *Bismillah*
under your breath
as they said *Amen*
during grace at Sunday dinners.
You wonder how many times
you've translated yourself.

Last New Year's Eve, you opened your home
to your friends, spent hours
making a playlist of '90s R&B songs
only to have your Palestinian friend
turn off your music because it was *haram.*
You wondered whether you were in your house
or his.

Even now, sitting in line for prayer,
you avoid calling the *adhan.* You remember
what your Saudi friends said:
You can only know God in Arabic.
You remember what your voice carries—
your long drawl, your black-eyed peas
and collard greens, your parents' Christianity.
It reveals your black neck, your familial
disconnect, your fried chicken breath.

"AMONG JINN AND MEN" [1]
-The Qur'an, Chapter 114, Verse 5

Have you ever seen your jinn?

I catch mine on the porch, breathing icy breath
into his hands. That blue-black, hunch-backed
trickster creeps around corners. I see him digging

under my house at night. A jinn that beams in the dark.
He appears, laughing behind my back,
follows me up the stairs and crawls into my bed.

Have you ever slept with your jinn?

Let him run his thin fingers through your hair,
pull strands through his teeth? His breath freezes
on my lips and a black tongue licks the frost away.

I awake wet, pale, bloodless blue, gasping for air.
He stands over me, eyes glaring back my very color.
I grab his hands, pin them to the bed.

Have you ever wrestled your jinn?

Drag him across your room, throw him
against the wall, hurl chairs and lamps
into thin air?

I stand for hours among the pieces
hot, thirsty, veins protruding, swearing
he was here, cursing the day I let him in.

SECURITY

I stood there, arms stretched up
and out, TSA officer patting me down.
I should have known better,
worn short sleeves, tighter jeans,
hot pink or baby blue, not brown, not black.
I should have pulled this hijab back
in a bun, worn hoop earrings, tried to appear
less foreign. I should have
let it fall, carried it like nothing,
a shawl. Instead, I chose habit
draped over ears, below my chin
and ignored the possibility
of not passing.

I watched her press my head, my neck,
behind my ears, my chest.
Just making sure, she said,
facing me, as if she could not see
through this curtain of difference.
She pressed and pressed, stared
and pressed, not wanting to believe
that I could be safe and Muslim.

TO MUSLIMS WHO DO NOT SAY, SALAAM

All your life, you've tried to muffle the sound
of your father trumpeting the adhan
in your ear every day, five times a day.
You've hung your mother in the closet
of your mind, ashamed of her habit. But a hijabi
walking toward you raises your dead,
and you must look away. You've white washed
your name, turned Abdullah to Abe, Suhaylah to Haley.
But here is faith, that security checkpoint
you thought you had already passed.
Will it set off the prayers resting in your palms,
the Arabic on your tongue? You look away
and do not say, **Peace**. Because how can you wish
for your sister what you do not have yourself?

I took a break from Arabic
cuz Arabic had broken me.
He taught from right to left;
I could never follow his lead.

Mus-ta-keen & dahhh-leen.
I had to get the verses down:
Ash-ha-du & ee-ya-ka-na-ba-du.
I tripped up over the sounds.

On every test, I mixed consonants
with vowels and read too slow.
I kept forgetting the next word;
his prayers were not my own.

I grew tired of counting beats
and translating my feelings.
Half the time, I didn't even know
what the hell I was sayin'.

When Arabic's back was turned,
I'd whip out my southern tongue:
God, come on over with some blessins'
OR, **Mane, you be trippin', son.**

Who is he to grade
how confession sounds?
I wanna hear a mix of notes.
I wanna say what's on my mind.

Arabic was tryin' to train me. I know.
But, I'll finish that class another day.
I took a break from Arabic
so I could pray my way.

SECTION 3

12.   Would my mother's hair still blow in the wind?

>   Its long, thick, black strands
>   would be curled under,
>   resting on her shoulders
>   nudged gently by a breeze
>   but would move more freely
>   when she'd throw her head back
>   in laughter, showing the crowns
>   on her teeth.

13.   Would my father still work in finance?

>   Perhaps Morgan Stanley
>   or maybe a small accounting firm
>   he started with a frat brother.
>   Or perhaps
>   he'd quit anyways
>   and rediscover his love
>   of Spanish, German, &
>   French, turn
>   out to be a teacher
>   anyways, his languages laced
>   as they are now
>   with mathematical phrases:
>   ***Vominos!*** Let's rise and run!
>   My ***liebe*** grows exponentially!
>   ***Bonne nuit***, my little dividend.

14.   How rich would we have been?

            Rich enough to travel
            to the ocean and back
            each summer
            no matter the deadline
            or meeting.

15.   When would they have given me my first sip of champagne?

            Right before my cotillion,
            they'd pour four glasses
            (one for Harold or Samuel)
            and make a toast
            to me.

16.   How would it feel to share my sisters' last name, to be known as one
        of Billy's kids?

            Like I was a part of history,
            an inside story, something
            recognizable.

my sister's suitcase is full of Texas—
one red step-in, two 60-minute phone cards,
three broken pearls,
past-due electric bills,
empty Mary Kay concealers,
Huggies, a picture of her husband
with his wives,
two state permits—
one for driving, the other to conceal
her .45.
wrapped in our father's letters,
all of which begin:
Patiently persevere.

POLYGAMY

My sister staggers in my direction.
Her body is the shape of a red apple.
I grab her suitcase from the conveyer;
Only had time to pack one bag, she says.
She insists on carrying her luggage;
I don't object.

Growing up, we spiked our hair and danced
to Prince in our bedroom mirror.
We both inherited Dad's weak eye;
hers always sagged more.
On the bus home, she rubs her stomach
in nervous circles, looks up every minute,
not sure she's really gotten away.
I wonder if her condition is contagious.

At home she unpacks:
five pairs of underwear, one black shoe,
three suit jackets, one pair of pants, a broken comb,
wedding pictures.
I think of the fun we'll have burning them all.

She had masked her four trips home—
"holidays" to get from under
that slick-tongued man
who loved women into submission.
Our family speaks in code now:
Glad you're back.
You're pregnant? Didn't know you were trying.
So, how long is your visit?
She sleeps to avoid answers.

I know she dreams of his wives.
Their faces stare back, indignant,
laughing like ghosts after a spook.

IDDAH: PART I
~the 3-month waiting period after a divorce

It's five in the morning, and Uzair is beating down
Asma's front door. She's still his wife.

> *Where is the baby, Asma? Get him*
> *before his father does.*

Uzair's wives welcomed Asma to the family.
They never felt burdened.

> *This month has been the first you've slept*
> *without the taste of other women on your tongue.*

Asma went to court without Uzair's word.
This divorce means nothing.

> *Where is your gun, Asma?*
> *No fooling around.*

It's five in the morning, and Asma's husband is kicking in
the front door. She is his wife, cowering in the basement.

> *The baby is crying upstairs. Breath heavy*
> *with milk—thick like his father's.*

Asma stopped visiting the mosque, won't return
his wives' calls. Wives should be sisters.

> *Asma, remember your voice—*
> *It is something to keep.*

After three months Asma will be single.
No man will take her in such hostility.

> *The gun is wrapped in a bundle—*
> *no, that is the baby.*

It's five thirty, and Asma's husband is swearing
in her bedroom. She is the wife crawling out a basement window.

The cries, bone deep.
No, Asma, don't stop to listen.

She wears *hijab* so the marks don't show.
She wears *hijab* so the *jihad* looks good.
She wears *hijab* 'til the black burns her skin.

*

If my sister could speak, she would breathe.

She sleeps up under a polygamist.

Who knows what he's got?

Her, him and the baby make three.

Who knows what she's got?

*

My sister's son has hands just like his daddy's.
We've both thought about burning them off.

She wraps the baby up under her scarf,
feeds him milk 'til teething draws blood.

*

She wears *hijab* so the marks don't show.
She wears *hijab* so the *jihad* looks good.
She wears *hijab* 'til she forgets the color she holds.

*

If my sister could speak, she would let me go first.

When the saleswoman hands me
a camisole over the fitting room door
and asks, **Why do you cover?**
I give my usual speech:
**Because it is an act of faith
a sign**, an ayah, **of modesty; my body—
a gift I unwrap for whom I please.**
She responds, **Oh, how beautiful!**

But as she leaves, I face myself
half-dressed, struggling to pull the garment
over chest. I want to open that door
and call after her: **The truth is
I cover because I always have,
afraid of what I will see—skin
& doubt. I cover so I don't have to think
about whether I truly believe.**

I stand in reflection. Hourglass curves
entice me to dream: a little black dress,
summer wind through hair.
In the honesty of day, I could turn heads
or be overlooked still.
I could risk it, step out
of this faith—Oh, God,
what would my husband say?

A knock on the door brings me back.
Does the garment not fit? the saleswoman asks.
It fits fine, I say. **But too much for me to pay.**
I lay it away, slip into my jacket
and reach for my hijab.
I pull it off the hook and drape it
overhead, pinning the performance in place.

Iddah: Part II

A girl on a couch by the window—
On the bed by the window is a girl—
On the bed, a girl—

The girl is a woman.

A woman is on the bed.
She is shaped like an apple.
The woman sleeps alone.

She's divorced.

The divorced woman sleeps
in yesterday's clothes—
The divorced woman lies
 in yesterday's clothes.

Her name is Asma.

Asma lies in yesterday's clothes
to keep from undressing.

Asma is your sister.

My sister lies on my bed
in yesterday's silk shirt and linen pants.
Her body a bruised apple.

Your body is not like your sister's.

My body is not like Asma's.
A bruised apple, she lies
on my bed in yesterday's shirt and pants,
anything to keep from undressing.

You are your sister's keeper.

I am my sister
lying on a bed
under a window,
bruised. I must keep her
and myself
out of yesterday's clothes.

THE DUBAI NEWS HEADLINE:
Woman Possessed by Jinn; Denies Husband[2]

I.

I am her husband. I have my right hand,
the Quran, and good intentions.
If her body had been taken,
I should have been told. I have rights
over her. Another's hands
have unearthed her soft jewels.
How can I touch her now?
I am my brother's joke. Cuckold.
Her bedroom door locked.
Each night another excuse,
I'm not able to pray, not feeling well, too sleepy.
Women's words. I know my rights,
but I tried sabr. **Patience**, her father suggested.
I spoke a word to the right. For a month,
I tiptoed, pretended not to hear
her strange conversations.
I even let her write her poetry.
I don't understand. Her body
grasped by another, right next to me.
She summoned him, I'm sure, to keep me
a dog in heat. She wanted to be free
of me. But I took her into marriage
with my right hand. Let her scream victim
if she must. I will claim what is my right.

II.

The court must have four witnesses
to rule **adultery**.
Our hands are tied. The Quran
is law. We can't hold her jinn
accountable, put him on trial.
We need a body to confirm
this betrayal. But fault can be laid
on the wife. She knew her jinn
and should have disclosed him
before she disrobed.
How could this man stay tied
to her when she is still tied
to her jinn? Must he remain intruded upon,
every night robbed of his basic dignity?
Divorce is allowed
in this case. The Quran is law.

III.

My jinn is my muse, a translator
of old tongues; together, we read ghazals
and parse Latin poems. I knew my husband
would never understand. Let him say
adultery. He doesn't know the word
I need to hear: **privacy**. I don't want to listen
to **rights**. I know my left hand, how to use it
to shut doors and trace images in moonlight.
I know new pronunciations, too. Marriage
is an outdated dictionary. Father tried to cover me,
give excuses for why I wouldn't share my bed,
this holy space of learning. He doesn't know
that knowledge is hard to take back
once created. My jinn is here; my hands are tied.
This I know.

In the Parking Lot of a Houston Wal-Mart

A woman pushes two boys
in an empty shopping cart.

                    The woman is tired.

Loud, frizzy-haired, dirty.
the boys fight; the woman digs
in her purse.

                    Marriage is expensive.

One boy pulls the other's hair.
He screams, bites
his brother's hand.

                    The boys are like their father—

In the parking lot of a Houston
Wal-Mart, a mother returns
with her sons.
People stare with raised brows.
They know.

                    The father is a polygamist.

The father has two more sons
by a second wife. He wants
all his sons to be brothers.

                    This woman doesn't want **his** family.

Her sons remind her of their father,
their other mother.
The woman has scrubbed dark blotches
on the boys' hands, stretched
their round cheeks, pressed
the curl of their hair.
The boys remain.

                    The woman can't keep those boys.

In the parking lot of a Houston
Wal-Mart, a mother returns
her sons.

ON THE DRIVE TO TEXAS TO PICK UP YOUR SON FROM HIS FATHER

you tell me you really wanted to say, **No,**
on your wedding day, but guests had arrived.

Sitting in the passenger's seat,
I turn to your face, see my weak eye

in yours. We are sisters, each other's garments,
but I am just seeing you uncovered.

You tell me you wanted to be a doula.
I never knew. You tell me how your husband

evaded the IRS, made deals under the table,
and kept his other wife a few doors down.

I never knew. You tell me you couldn't come home
and face questions alone. I tell you I understand

how hard it is to be tied to someone
and remember yourself. We are sisters

both afraid of changing our minds,
of letting go of images—a ring around a finger,

a faith sitting so snug.
After we arrive, you surprise me

with tickets to the Prince concert,
a thank-you for making the trip.

I had never been to a concert before.
That night, I watch you primp,

compare my flats and jeans
to your heels and wrap dress.

I watch you strut to our seats.
You were always curves and confidence.

During the show, you watch Prince
finger his guitar strings, spin

and split, lick his lips. I watch you
sing back, jump out your wounds and dance

like everyone is looking. I swear
this is the type of sister I want to be.

I set down my purse, put my hands
in the air and roll my hips.

I don't know the words, and you don't care.
We do the bump and scream lose our fears.

The next day, we meet your husband
outside a bank. You don't say hello

but take your son, buckle him in
and drive away for the last time.

He whines the entire trip home.
With each note, you grind your teeth

and I turn up the music from last night's CD,
my way of helping you & myself

remember the night, bass and body, things
we've always had but never knew.

SECTION 4

DUTY

Each morning, your alarm rings
and you rise, intent and deliberate.
Your lean body stretches itself of sleep,
embracing the inevitable day.
I am sure I have married my father.
I duck under covers, burrow my head
back into night and interrupted dreams.
I have not yet become my mother.
For years, she rose like mercury,
fashioned my father toast and two eggs
sunny-side up, ironed his shirts, packed his lunch,
saw him off to work. Each morning,
I fail to convince my body
to become your wife. Sleep always lures
with possibilities, untold stories.
Hours later, I wake, wild-haired,
sprawled across the bed.
You are gone, and I, alone, always regret
how easily I shut out the sun.

Aisha (noun): 1. Alive; full of life.

Last month, I dreamt I stood on a precipice
pulling my hijab off a bush with no leaves.
The hijab resisted like a woman not wanting to be taken
into the arms of a man. There, under blue-red sky,
we wrestled. I tried to tie her. She hoped to free herself
as if she didn't know my touch, my very name.

A friend said when a woman dreams of being
without her hijab, her husband will leave her.

Aisha (noun): 2. Prosperous

Later, we met with a marriage counselor.
You said I hold grudges, so busy twisting
your every word out of shape. Love would be so simple
if I just stopped fighting. That night, I dreamt
my hijab and I neared the edge. She sighed, Bismillah—
In the Name of God—then poured herself into my hands.

My friend said it was a good thing
my dream ended like this.

Aisha (noun): 3. The Prophet's Wife

Over plates of sushi, you ask me how I feel
being out in public without my hijab.
I say I don't feel any different than when I'm at home—
raw, unhooked, completely natural.

You smile, reassure me of hijab's beauty,
her ability to make a woman
Muslim, to make her husband
even. You love me and I you.
I let you eat the last salmon roll,
its pink flesh peeking out,
and wonder how to truly unwrap myself.

17.   Would I dance like no one is watching?

        To twerk or not to twerk—
        that is the question.

18.   A one-piece or bikini on the beach?

        A bikini,
        to feel the wind wrap
        around my waist, an embrace
        that fills in gaps.

19.   Would I have married my husband?

        I would have been pulled
        into another's arms,
        known nothing
        of how ticklish he is
        behind his ears,
        how he talks of flying
        in his sleep,
        of how he covers
        his psoriasis
        in the sun.
        I would have known
        nothing of how he was raised
        with a Muslim father
        and a Christian mother,
        would not have learned
        the courage it takes
        to adopt one parent's faith
        and still balance love
        for them both.

REMEMBRANCE

If anyone withdraws from remembrance
Of God we appoint for him
An evil one to be an intimate companion
    — The Quran, Chapter 43, Verse 36

My jinn knocks at my door.
How could I not answer, turn away
his grin? He takes off his shoes,
unbuttons his shirt, and starts undoing
every flower, every smile,
my husband's kisses, & all my prayers.
What an affair. This jinn unveils.
Each whisper, a hand slipping off faith.
Why can't I lock that door, stop
entertaining doubt? Let God wrap His hands
around me, expel my jinn, his stories,
and believe in this body? If I could, I would pray:
No God but God. I know not,
and you are the knower of all hidden things.

the tissue in my left breast would crack,
like someone was pulling apart
a peeled orange.
I would move my body
so whatever was wrong would pop
back into place.
Doctors say some women
are more prone to cysts.

**You just have to wait
until they come.**

After surgery, they bandaged my breast
with white cotton patches. The pressure
stretched my skin like over-inflated balloons.
I pulled back the sticky cloth to see stitches,
railroad tracks whose grooves sunk deep.

I feared the day I would uncover
the markings to a lover.
He would frown
at the wrinkled skin around my nipple.

A year later, the cyst reappeared.
They had to dig further,
push aside all the scar tissue.
I could feel the doctor tug
as she threaded the needle through the old wound.
Sometimes the scar tissue burns,
like it's slicing through the weight
of my breast. Other times, it throbs, tired
from bubbling up a new knot
that sits anxious against the wall.

Last night, I told my husband I wanted to have a baby.
I don't want a baby. I just want to be held.
I want to be wrapped in his arms. I want
to be sung to. I want a song. I want a book
to read, to write, to rock me to sleep.
I don't want a damn baby. I want to be
looked after. Pampered. The first thing on his list.
Kissed. Dress ripped. Off. Once. Twice.
Three times a day. Where is that birth control?
I want him to stop saving everybody in the streets
and save me. Keep me. Like a poem. I want him
to read my poems. Want him to write a poem.
To be a poem. My poem. Inside of me.

YOU TRY TO BRING FLOWERS
~for my husband

When sky dawns, you rise
and rush to stand before God.
I wake in envy.

You open shutters,
bring in sun. I shut shutters.
Never asked for that much sun.

Silly boy. Who pats
sand into castles just as
water rushes in?

I pick at your weeds
because I am scared to tend
the jasmine in mine.

AL-TARIQ THE NIGHT STAR

And what will explain to thee
what the night visitant is?
(It is) the Star
of piercing brightness.
            -The Quran, Chapter 86, Verses 1-3

Against the night and its heavy curtain,
Tariq keeps God's light.

Before the dawn weaves its white thread,
open windows, let this night visitor in.

Every soul has its Tariq – the brilliance
and faith that appear only in shadows.

Such a coy lover, Tariq lays light into palms,
blankets the anxious body, leaves longing.

Why must His light always fade? Cyclical
presence, distant body I could never grasp.

If the crescent moon and night star are signs of God,
then let me be the moon to have His star in my curve.

A Dua[3] Before Making Love

Embrace your body.
Touch it. Let him love it. What
are you waiting for?

to my left breast that proves my strength
to the widow's peak I thread back
to my right eyebrow arched from knowing
to my freckles, memories browned by sun
to my sleepy eye, heavy with secrets
to my nose that sits a bell
to admitting beauty in all of this

To Mother You Again...

I wear you into the sun
that first July. I take you from
my mother's house
unswaddle your limbs, let you breathe
& stretch into yourself.
The wind will carry your colic away,
I tell myself.
We walk with no place to go.
You feel my shoulders lower,
my arms loosen. I breathe
and you smile finally.

We move back to our house.
I make room for you.
I open the shutters and convert
your bassinet to a full crib. I push back
the couch, sit you up on the floor,
turn on music and dance
again. I share you with the world.
I bring you to dinner parties and play dates,
and post pictures of me laughing.
I tell myself I am beautiful.
I tell you you are beautiful.

In this I teach us both how to trust
ourselves, how to imagine
our own freedom,
a song with no words.

SECTION 5

20.   Could I imagine a woman playing sports fully covered?

> I volleyed,
> hit overheads,
> lobbed, sliced
> my left-handed serve
> out-wide, & played
> split sets wearing sweats
> and long sleeves
> in summer heat.
> Match point.

21.   Would I know how to get away with a bad hair day, every day?

> Listen, non-Muslim ladies,
> you have to get a real scarf,
> not an old t-shirt
> or a piece of fabric
> with frayed ends.
> That's the shit
> you sleep in.

22.   How easy would it have been to join in those middle school taunts?

> Towel head!
> Cancer girl!
> Dirty Muslim!

23. Would my mother know the fine art of substitution?

> Turkey pepperoni, turkey sausage,
> turkey links, turkey patties, turkey hotdogs,
> chicken sausage, alcohol-free eggnog,
> O'DOUL'S, halal marshmallows.

24. Would I know the sweet relief of a date during Ramadan?

> It's deceiving,
> that brown, wrinkled
> thumb. It's wrapped
> in a thin pastry skin,
> yet holds a chewy interior.
> Its body signals an end
> to a day's worth
> of hunger and
> penitence, hand-held
> spiritual satisfaction.

25. What would my father have told me on 9/11?

> That evening, he reminded,
> **Dare to be different**
> and I, away at college, knew
> it did not mean
> covering.
> It meant revealing
> myself
> like he did
> when he left
> his father's faith
> and fate. I understood

that night
that just by being,
I was making a name
for myself.

How could I forget my mother,
her nails painted grapefruit red every week,
her trips to Nordstrom for a new pair
of open-toed heels, sling-backs, and wedges
that she matched perfectly with her hijabs?
How could I not recall her strutting
in the masjid in her diamond studded jeans?
Her love of Tresor perfume? My mother knew
how to keep herself together in this faith.
She taught me how to balance two worlds:
how to fry fish in steamy masjid kitchens
and where to place the wine glass and soup spoon
on a proper dinner table. She passed down
her mother's slips and camisoles, opera gloves
and mink stoles, turned Sunday hats
into Friday tams, switched between hot combs
and hijab pins, followed Arabic classes
with piano lessons by uncle Arthur.
How could I not remember how she posed
at the Peabody club's Christmas brunch,
a glass of sparkling cider in one hand,
her Swarovski clutch in the other,
toe out, hip to the side,
then thikred after prayer that night?
She'd caravanned to Detroit and Atlanta,
those meccas of black Muslims,
but kept summers for grandparents in St. Louis
where she braided and beaded my hair,
let me run free and never apologized
for the freedom of conversion.

Wear your hijab. Make sure it's tucked tight. Pin it up so your neck doesn't sweat. Cock it to the side. Wear your heels. Go with your girlfriend. Not the one who's never been to the club before. She'll constantly remind you she's never been to the club before. Go with the one you saw pop and lock it that one time in the mosque. Pick a club where you can actually dance. Not grind. But dance. Step in all fierce like Grace Jones and dare anyone to tell you there's no hijab allowed in the club. Why shouldn't you? Find a spot on the dance floor. Claim it. Twerk. But don't get all #teamtwerkchampion in the club. You're still a hijabi in the club. Let your hijab work for you. Let it ward off the guy who just wants to hit and quit. Forget those men at the mosque who say this is **haram**. Dance! Hold on to that bass in your hips. Why shouldn't you? Go to the bar and order a Sprite. Repeat the word **Sprite** when the bartender looks at you funny. Tell him you're the designated driver. When you see another Muslim at the club, let's say, Mahmood, raise your cup and give him the **Salaams**. You're still a Muslim at the club. Who cares what he thinks? He's at the club, too. Dance, girl! Look at your watch. Isha prayer time—and you're at the club. But you decided to go to the club, so be at the club. Make peace with the music in the moment. When the DJ plays your favorite song, throw up your hands and yell, **That's my jam!** Dance. You're there in the club, hijab and all, not pretending or denying or lying. Remember, Allah sees all. So, dance and don't look down. Why shouldn't you?

All those letters, waiting to be turned. One by one
by one, you expect me to touch their skin, walk that stage,
clap as if the letters uncovered themselves, but I'm the one turning **A**—no,
D—hoping a square lights my memory. Word-making isn't
easy. But you say I must remember orders, places, faces. N-E-V-E-R
forget the details. Mother always said the devil is in the details, said
guessing won't do for her daughter. I must measure each word, stride,
hair-do, and dress. All those dresses! Rhinestone, sheath, empire waist.
I'm a model employee, a mother's dream. I do as I'm told.
Just say the W-O-R-D. ***Make sense out of missing pieces***, mother would say,
Keep things straight: iron the collar first, dessert spoon above the
Lenox plate, hand-wash your delicates. The details! Sometimes I forget
my own voice. Yes, I asked to be seen, but I can't pretend I don't
need to be heard. I can guess words too, can C-A-L-L them
out, but I must be silent, hold back K-N-O-W-L-E-D-G-E, watch while
Pat teaches, answers behind the guardrail, able to taunt,
question contestants. I want to spin that wheel, let it stop wherever,
risk a turn, even bankruptcy. I'll trade this fame to D-I-S-R-E-G-U-A-R-D
syntax, buy a consonant, steal an opponent's letter, give up
these titles: side-kick, model, letter-turner-turned actress.
Uniqueness has its price. But you made me a joke, a cute Mexican tune - ***Oh***
Vanna, Pick me a letter. Comedy fashions me a robot, parodied by that
Weird Al. T-A-K-E B-A-C-K this glitz and glamour, this Hollywood
X-tra ordinary, all these details. Here is your scalpel, your fountain of
Youth, purchased, pulled and tucked. I'll trade your Ps and Qs for
Z's, a restful sleep, a future of unfilled spaces. I want to solve my own puzzle.

Hijab be talkin' back.
Hijab be talkin' Black.
Hijab be runnin' thangs.
Hijab be like, *What you say?*
Hijab be sayin', *Watch me work.*
Hijab be meanin', *Watch me flirt.*
Hijab be prayin' still.
Hijab be raisin' hell.
Hijab be like, *Get outta my way.*
Hijab be all up in yo' face.
Hijab be southern and sweet.
Hijab be sun-kissed sweet tea.
Hijab be smilin', *Yes, ma'am.*
Hijab be battin' them eyes, *Salaam.*
Hijab be knowin' how I feel.
Hijab be like, *Just hold still.*
Hijab be coverin' my sin.
Hijab be layin' it on thick.
Hijab be turnin' all sullen and blue.
Hijab be swearin' she don't look good.
Hijab be tired of the spotlight.
Hijab be like, *I ain't comin' out tonight.*
Hijab be knowin' when she come round.
Hijab be takin' her time.
Hijab be ignorin' what you say.
Hijab be rearrangin' her place.
Hijab be like, *Take me or leave me.*
Hijab be any thang she wannabe.

you pray. Let her grab your hand like you do hers.
Let her lead you away from bills and tests and texts

and into submission. Web her chubby little fingers
through yours as you step down stairs

one by one, over sippy cups & blocks, past spilled cereal
and muddy socks to reach that quiet space

where you once retreated when your faith
was young, uncluttered & easy.

You've since closed those doors. How can you return
with your depression, failed

ventures, gained weight, hands shaking?
How can you stand to hear your voice

tremble? But your daughter
is leading you: *you cannot run from this.*

Let her pull those blue scarves lying
on the edge of the desk. Help her drape hers

as you drape yours. This is mothering.
Stand by her side when she cups her jelly-covered hands

like she saw you do months ago. Life
has not broken you.

Smile. What a blessing memory is,
precise as her hands folded over each other.

Remember, your mother showed you
prayer, how to bend and rise,

how fall to your knees. *Alhumdullilah.*
This is how you learned your body

can be a vessel of gratitude. Your daughter is learning
hers now. Let her crawl onto your back

as you place your head to the floor. *Subhanallah.*
Listen to her giggle jumbled words you once uttered.

Let them stir up verses you forgot, that you let sit
dormant, a potted plant, wilted in shadow.

Rise. What made you forget the strength of your legs
to pull you back up after falling?

Raise your hands to ears, summon the words
you always silence, *Allahuakbar!*

Smile. Bend your toes. Feel your spirit spread
like ivy. Know that she sees you come back. Your hands

hugged under your breasts. This is what daughters do.
They remind you of yourself.

IF MY DAUGHTER DOES NOT WEAR HIJAB

My daughter's hair grows black.
Its curls are thick and wild,
the roots soft and wavy,
the ends rough and tangled.

I could straighten it, smooth it out
like my mother did mine
each Saturday by the kitchen stove,
tie a scarf over it at 11 years old.

Or maybe I will stand in awe
of her crown of curls, adorn it
with pink bows. Let it poof
in humidity, let it grow

into itself. Her hair holds faith and questions
together just as any hijab could.
Each kink—her way of wrestling
with God.

Daughters will always twist themselves
anew. I cut my hair, switched between
hoodies and hijabs, stopped praying
at mega-mosques.

My daughter will uncover herself too
and I will help her—oil her scalp,
her own ablution, make a puff ball
or plait, French braid or afro.

Each style, a new supplication.
And I will send her off to the world
& tell her, **This, too, is witness.**

[1]The jinn are spiritual beings made of smokeless fire, neither angels nor devils. They have free will and can inhabit the earth in a physical form, acting as somewhat of a trickster for the purposes of good or evil. Every human is said to have a jinn. The Prophet Muhammad was said to have made his jinn Muslim.

[2]In 2014, a Dubai man divorced his wife after she continuously denied him sex. The wife's family claims that the jinn possessed the woman. The Dubai courts granted the husband the divorce and initially required him to pay alimony but later freed him of this obligation, ruling that because the wife did not disclose that she was possessed by the jinn she did not deserve financial support (BBC News, 17 October 2014, "UAE: Man divorces wife 'possessed by genie'").

[3]A supplication in which the speaker cups his/her hands together.

With thanks to the editors of the following publications in which these poems first appeared.

Callaloo: "A Hijab of My Own"

CALYX Journal: "Layl-tul-Qadr"

Crab Orchard Review: "To The White Boy Who Pulled Off My Hijab in 7th Grade Gym" and "The Fitting Room"

Halal If You Hear Me: "Accent" and "Hot Combs and Hijabs"

Muslim WakeUp!: "Iddah"

Mythium: "In the Parking Lot of a Houston Wal-Mart"

Rattle: "Why I Can Dance Down A Soul Train Line and Still Be Muslim"

Sapelo Square: "To Muslims Who Do Not Say, 'Salaam'"

Tidal Basin Review: "Security"

Touchstone: "Under Veils" and "When I Was 13"

A very special thank you to my family: to my parents, you stepped out and spoke the truth of your belief and taught me that I can do the same, and through you, I learned how to own my background and create a path reflective of that; to my siblings, thank you for walking down this path with me, sharing your experiences, and letting me write through our adolescence and adulthood; to my extended family, thank you for showing me how faith and love blend beyond religious lines!

I am indebted to the following communities: Masjid Al-Muminun in Memphis, Tennessee which has served (and continues to serve) as a holy space for me, my family and friends, allowing us to exist as Black and Muslim, dancing and all!; the instructors and peers in my undergraduate and graduate creative writing programs at Rhodes College and Indiana University, respectively, for pushing me to write my experience and to complicate how I display it; to Cave Canem for birthing many of the poems in this manuscript and celebrating Black poetry; to my Kansas City writing community, Natasha and Gustavo, for workshopping and organizing this book, as well advising me on publishing. I am indebted to your honest, insightful feedback.

And I must give so much love to my husband for being my biggest supporter. Your positivity, faith, and encouragement have been constant and motivating! Thank you for pushing me to dive in! I love you!

Thank you to SparkWheel Press for seeing the beauty of this book and honoring its trajectory and voice. Thank you for being great collaborators.

ABOUT THE AUTHOR

Aisha Sharif is a Cave Canem fellow whose poetry has appeared in *Rattle*, *Callaloo*, *Crab Orchard Review*, *Tidal Basin Review*, and *Calyx*. She earned her MFA in Creative Writing at Indiana University, Bloomington and her BA in English from Rhodes College in Memphis, TN.

The poems in Aisha Sharif's *To Keep from Undressing* remind readers that Muslim narratives, bodies, and lineages don't just matter; they make up the American fabric, both historic and contemporary. Her poems show us that woven within that fabric is a tradition rooted in the same ideals and morals and complications as all other American narratives. Sharif's poems deconstruct the hijab not for metaphoric purposes, or to serve as a simplified how-to manual for the unlearned. The hijab becomes a directional marker into the poet herself, wondering "how to truly unwrap myself." And what we find is the good work of poetry: desire, regret, mis-spoken languages, vulnerabilities.

Mispronunciation and mistakes carry a lifetime of questions, and what makes this debut so remarkable is that every poem will ask questions without fear. Every poem asks its readers to sift through what made you; asks to take a good look at it all. When you repackage your personal history or a lesson, will you and your children see opportunity, or courage? Will you see all the reasons for joy to happen?

American Muslims and Islam, whether conversion or orthodox, are not tangential mythologies merely draped over an America arm. Their narratives don't need broadcasting to look at their uniqueness. Sharif's poems offer a true to life experience of American Muslims, and are "black skin glistened from sun." Sharif is a poet delivering the American journey with pride and honor, with boldness, "bass and body, things we've always had but never knew." Aisha Sharif has given the world such a marvelous collection of poems. To Keep from Undressing is the book we all need, as we learn (and relearn) how to continuously love ALL of ourselves, embracing that "This, too, is witness."

—**F. Douglas Brown**, author of *ICON*, and *Zero to Three*, winner of 2013 Cave Canem Poetry Prize

To Keep from Undressing, Aisha Sharif's timely debut collection, reveals the type of honesty that gets you uninvited to family reunions. Sharif requires honesty, not only of those she speaks of in her poems, but also of herself. The undressing comes from the wrestling with the truth of the discomfort but also the beauty of what we now call intersectionality but what has been long known as being a black woman in Americ—a folding and unfolding, a combination of internalized faith, motherhood, men, family and unshakable identity. In her collection, Sharif takes us just to the edge of danger, we peek over while covering our eyes and she even dangles us further than what is comfortable, only to return us to safety knowing we can never unsee the complexity of her intersectionality and what it means for us if we too are brave.

—**Natasha Ria El-Scari**, author of *The Only Other*

In nature, the greatest richness appears at the edges between habitat zones— between meadow and forest, oasis and desert, sea and shore. The same can be true of poetry that explores the edges between seemingly disparate realms or rival qualities, as in this fine collection by Aisha Sharif. She speaks in these poems of how it feels to be both Muslim and black, faithful and doubting, obedient and rebellious. Is wearing the hijab a sign of modesty or of subservience? Is praying in her own dialect as valid as praying in Arabic? How might her life be different if her parents had not converted from Christianity? The effort to fashion a coherent self amid these tensions and questions charges every page with energy.

—**Scott Russell Sanders**, author of *Earth Works*

It's not every day a reader is offered such an honest and unguarded look into the innermost thoughts of a Black Muslim woman. From the intersection of Black culture and religion, to conversations with jinn, to motherhood, marriage and the meaning of hijab, *To Keep From Undressing* beautifully melds private and public, interweaving bold and delicate themes into a one-of-kind tapestry of words and freeing truths. The reading experience is just as therapeutic to the reader as the writing was for the writer. That is the mark of pure magic.

—**Nadirah Angail**, author of *On All Things That Make Me Beautiful* and *What We Learned Along the Way*

CPSIA information can be obtained
at www.ICGtesting.com
Printed in the USA
JSHW021214090120
3468JS00001B/9